AS Physical Education
UNIT 1

Edexcel

Unit 1: The Social Basis of Sport and Recreation

Philip Allan Updates
Market Place
Deddington
Oxfordshire
OX15 0SE

tel: 01869 338652
fax: 01869 337590
e-mail: sales@philipallan.co.uk
www.philipallan.co.uk

© Philip Allan Updates 2005

ISBN-13: 978-1-84489-012-5
ISBN-10: 1-84489-012-0

This Guide has been written specifically to support students preparing for the Edexcel AS Physical Education Unit 1 examination. The content has been neither approved nor endorsed by Edexcel and remains the sole responsibility of the author.

Printed by MPG Books, Bodmin

Environmental information
The paper on which this title is printed is sourced from managed, sustainable forests.

Contents

Introduction

■ ■ ■

Content Guidance

■ ■ ■

Questions and Answers

Introduction

About this guide

This guide is written to help you to prepare for the Edexcel AS Physical Education Unit 1 examination, which covers the **Social Basis of Sport and Recreation**. The unit will also form part of the A2 assessment, with some of the material being re-examined in the synoptic examination.

This **Introduction** provides guidance on revision, together with advice on approaching the examination itself.

The **Content Guidance** section gives a point-by-point description of all the facts you need to know and concepts you need to understand for Unit 1. Although these are explained where necessary, you must be prepared to use other resources in your preparation. In this unit you will investigate the cultural background of sport and recreation in the UK and Europe. You will also investigate the social factors that influence both performance and participation.

The **Questions and Answers section** shows you the sort of questions you can expect in the unit examination. It would be impossible to give examples of every kind of question in one book, but these should give you a flavour of what to expect. Each question has been attempted by two candidates, Candidate A and Candidate B. Their answers, along with the examiner's comments, should help you to see what you need to do to score high marks — and how you can easily *not* score marks even though you probably understand the subject of physical education.

What can I assume about the guide?

You can assume that:
- the topics described in the Content Guidance section correspond to those in the specification
- the basic facts you need to know are stated clearly
- the major concepts you need to understand are explained
- the questions at the end of the guide are similar in style to those that will appear in the unit examination
- the answers supplied are genuine and not concocted by the author
- the standard of marking is broadly equivalent to that which will be applied to your unit test answers

What can I *not* assume about the guide?

You must not assume that:
- every last detail has been covered

- the way in which the concepts are explained is the only way in which they can be presented in an examination
- the range of question types presented is exhaustive (examiners are always thinking of new ways to test a topic)

So how should I use this guide?

The guide lends itself to a number of uses throughout your physical education course — it is not just a revision aid. Because the Content Guidance is laid out in sections that correspond to those of the specification for Unit 1, you can use it:

- to check that your notes cover the material required by the specification
- to identify strengths and weaknesses
- as a reference for homework and internal tests
- to help you write your local and national assignment in Unit 2 of the specification
- during your revision to prepare 'bite-sized' chunks of related material, rather than being faced with a file full of notes

The Questions and Answers section can be used to:

- identify the terms used by examiners in questions and what these expect of you
- familiarise yourself with the style of questions you can expect
- identify the ways in which marks are lost or gained

Preparing for the Unit 1 test

Preparation for examinations is a very personal thing. Different people prepare, equally successfully, in different ways. The key is being totally honest about what actually *works* for *you*. This is not necessarily the same as the style you would like to adopt. It is no use preparing to a background of loud music if this distracts you. Taking a sporting analogy, the practice environment should mirror the competitive one — for you this is the examination room.

Whatever your style, you must have a revision plan. Sitting down the night before the examination with a file full of notes and a textbook does not constitute an effective plan — it is just desperation! Whatever your personal style of revision, there are a number of strategies you *must* adopt and others you could consider.

What you *must* do

- Leave yourself enough time to cover *all* the material identified in the Unit 1 specification.
- Make sure that you actually have all the material to hand (use this book as a basis).
- Identify weaknesses early in your preparation so that you have time to do something about them.
- Familiarise yourself with the terminology used in the examination questions.

What you *could* do

- Copy selected sections of your notes.
- Summarise your notes into a more compact format, including the key points.
- Create your own flash cards — key points written on postcards (carry them around with you for quick revision during a coffee break or while sitting on the bus).
- Make audio recordings of your notes and/or the key points and play these back.
- Make a PowerPoint presentation of the key points and use this to revise in the last few days before the unit test.
- Discuss a topic with a friend who is studying the same course.
- Try to explain a topic to someone *not* following the course.
- Practise examination questions on the topic.

Approaching the Unit 1 test

Terms used in examination questions

You will be asked precise questions in the examination, so you can save valuable time — as well as ensuring you score as many marks as possible — by knowing what is expected. Terms most commonly used are explained below.

Brief

This means that only a short statement of the main points is required.

Define

This requires you to state the meaning of a term, without using the term itself.

Describe

This is a request for factual detail about a structure or process expressed logically and concisely.

Discuss

You are required to give a critical account of various viewpoints and arguments on the topic set, drawing attention to their relative importance and significance.

Evaluate

This means that a judgement of evidence and/or arguments is required.

Explain

This means that reasons have to be included in your answer.

Identify

This requires a word, phrase or brief statement to show that you recognise a concept or theory in an item.

List

This requires a sequence of numbered points, one below the other, with no further explanation.

Outline

This means give only the main points, i.e. don't go into detail. Don't be tempted to write more than necessary — this will waste time.

State

A brief, concise answer, without reasons, is required.

Suggest

This means that the question has no fixed answer, so a wide range of reasonable responses is acceptable.

What is meant by...?

This usually requires a definition. The amount of information needed is indicated by the mark allocation.

In the examination

When you finally open the test paper, it can be quite a stressful moment. You may not recognise the diagram or quote used in question 1. It can be quite demoralising to attempt a question at the start of an examination if you are not feeling very confident about it. However, remember that you have a lot of choice. Read all the questions carefully before deciding which to attempt. Other strategies for the examination itself include the following:

- *Do not* begin to write as soon as you open the paper.
- *Do not* necessarily answer question 1 first (the examiner did not sequence the questions with your particular favourites in mind).
- *Do* read all the questions before you start your answers.
- *Do* identify and answer first those questions about which you feel most confident, regardless of their order in the paper.
- *Do* remember to spend time planning your essay in Section B.
- *Do* read the question carefully — if you are asked to explain, then explain, don't just describe.
- *Do* take notice of the mark allocation and try to match this to the number of points you make in your answer.
- *Do* try to stick to the point in your answer (it is easy to stray into related areas that will not score marks and use up valuable time).
- *Do* make sure you fulfil the examination rubric, i.e. answer the correct number of questions from the right sections.

Content
Guidance

This section is a guide to **Unit 1: The Social Basis of Sport and Recreation**. The main areas covered are:

- concepts and definitions
- cultural background
- the development of physical education
- social influences on performance and participation
- professional (elite) sport
- recreative sport (mass participation)
- the Olympic Games: history and philosophy
- the Olympic issues

You may already be familiar with some of the information in these topic areas. However, it is important that you know and understand this information exactly as described in the specification. This summary of the specification content highlights key points and you should find it useful when revising for the Unit 1 test.

Concepts and definitions

Key points

Sports share the following characteristics:
- They involve competition against opponents where the aim is to win.
- They involve physical activity and all competitors have a chance of winning or losing.
- They have written rules and are played within set constraints of time and space.

Participation in sports can bring both **extrinsic** and **intrinsic rewards**. Extrinsic rewards, such as trophies and medals, are given by another person. Intrinsic rewards are personal feelings, such as pride and satisfaction.

Leisure is free time, i.e. when we are not working or fulfilling other obligations, such as eating and sleeping. It is a personal concept — the key is that people are free to choose their own activities. Although there have always been some forms of leisure throughout history, we now have more free time and can choose from a far greater range of activities.

Recreation is the positive use of free time. Physical recreation includes exercise. Recreation tends to promote intrinsic rewards for the performer.

Key concepts you must understand

A basic classification of sports includes invasion games, target games, striking/ fielding games, combat sports, aquatic activities and outdoor recreation.

Invasion games, such as rugby and football, involve teams invading an opponent's territory. The origin of invasion games lies in the mob games of the pre-industrial period, where one part of the community played against another. Target games, such as archery, involve the use of marksmanship and have clear origins in war and defence. Striking/fielding games, such as cricket and rounders, involve teams competing to score the highest number of runs or points. They are unique in that an individual batsman/batter from one team plays against the whole fielding team of the opposition.

Combat sports are the oldest type of sports; they involve a range of activities including boxing, wrestling and fencing. They were used to help people prepare for war in bygone years. Aquatic activities, such as swimming and sailing, were also functional in their origin.

Outdoor recreation takes place in the natural environment and is associated with challenge and a degree of risk. These types of activity have experienced a boom in recent years. This expansion is linked to the greater availability of transport, and developments in technology, which mean that specialist equipment and clothing required are easier to get hold of and cheaper. Increasing media coverage, especially on extreme sports channels, has also helped to develop the popularity of these activities.

Cultural background

Key points

- The importance of combat sports (linked to medieval knights and preparation for war).
- Festival games and the role of the church, court and peasant.
- Popular recreation activities — you will need to describe two or three named examples.
- Characteristics of games played in the pre-industrial phase.
- Characteristics of pre-industrial society.
- Differences between gentry and peasant sport (real tennis versus mob football).
- Patronage of the church and local gentry.

Combat sports and the gentry

Most early sports were used in preparation for war or to develop hunting skills, and because of this many are referred to as combat sports. The Norman Conquest of 1066 formed a new social order in England, creating a landed gentry and a subservient peasant class. Combat sports followed this division. This was a period of instability and war, and there was a need for all men to maintain their fighting fitness.

The young gentry were the knights — an elite band who spent years developing their fighting and horsemanship skills to fulfil this honour. The main focus for their sporting training was the joust and the tournament.

'Tournament' was a generic term used to describe games of knightly skills. Its earliest form was the **tourney** — a meeting of two teams of knights on a designated field of combat, often with miles of varying terrain — in a free-for-all or mêlée. It was like scheduling a small war for sport and was highly dangerous.

Tourneys were gradually replaced by the smaller and less brutal **jousts**. These took place in confined areas (royal showgrounds), often with purpose-built grandstands to allow spectators to watch the action.

The greatest attractions of the tournament were the colour, pageantry and social life. After the invention of gunpowder, which made the heavily armoured horseman out-of-date, it was these aspects of the entertainment that became most important.

Archery and the peasant classes

Archery was a requisite military skill for the lower classes. The longbow was an essential part of English military strategy, being simpler and having greater rapidity of fire than the crossbow. A succession of English kings made it compulsory for all men to own a bow and to practise on Sundays. Some banned all other pastimes and recreations. Archery practice and competition were commonly undertaken at butts, which were often established in churchyards.

Festival games

The time available for sport was often restricted to holy days. Travel was difficult and so recreation activities were local and used ready-to-hand materials. Recreation activities changed through the year. In the winter, mass games such as mob football were played. These were often violent contests with few rules. In the summer, gentler, more individual and athletic-type activities were followed.

The year began with spring fertility festivals, although some games took place as early as New Year's Day and Plough Monday (the first Monday after Christmas). Most, however, focused on Easter. Shrove Tuesday was a particularly popular day for violent mob games, especially forms of football. May Day was often marked by games in which young men chased women, again concerned with rituals of fertility. Whitsuntide was the high point of the sporting year, with much dancing and games. This was a slack time for agriculture, and crops and animals were left to grow! Summer games tended to be gentler — running, jumping and throwing contests. The church provided space to play, often offered patronage to games and festivals, and may have donated prizes.

Gentry recreations

Having access to land, resources and leisure time allowed the upper classes to develop a wider range of recreational sports. Obvious examples include the various types of hunting and horse sports that also served as social occasions. In terms of games, these were usually individual or small-sided. Court games were sophisticated in terms of both equipment and systems of scoring. This was in direct contrast to the mob games played by the lower classes. The most popular court game was real or royal tennis, played on a purpose-built indoor court. Real tennis epitomised the exclusivity of these types of games.

What the examiners will expect you to be able to do

- Discuss the importance of the link between combat sports and knights' preparation for war.
- Describe the pre-industrial festival games and the role of the church, court and peasant classes.
- Identify the differences between gentry and peasant sport.
- Explain the patronage of the church and local gentry and their support for sport.

Tip You need to try to remember around eight key points to answer questions on both pre-industrial and post-industrial sport. Make a list of these points and see if you can make a mnemonic to help you remember them (a mnemonic is a word or phrase made up by using the first letter of all the key words).

The development of physical education

Sport in post-industrial Britain

Key points

- The development of sport after 1800.
- The impact of changes in society on the development of sport.
- The effect of the three key revolutions: industrial, transport and urban.

Codification and administration

Sport in the post-industrial phase is characterised by the development of **codification** and **administration**.

Codification involved the creation and maintenance of a set of national rules. The developing transport system meant that teams and individuals could travel out of their local areas to compete on a national scale. This highlighted the problem of local versions of games and local rules. In most cases, each sport appointed a national governing body (NGB) which standardised the rules for the sport. The NGBs then began to develop more regular fixtures and competitions.

After the Industrial Revolution, most people lived and worked in urban areas and the influence of the rural elements from the popular recreation era steadily declined. (Modern sport is also urban sport.)

There were a number of changes in the way people lived and worked that had an influence on sport in the post-industrial period:
- **Urbanisation** meant large populations moving into cities and towns where there was a lack of space for recreation.
- **Industrialisation** led to life based around the factory system and machine time. The old saints' days and holy days were largely lost and work was no longer organised around the seasons — every week was a busy time.
- **Working conditions** initially were very poor for the lower classes, with long shifts and little free time. The twentieth century saw a gradual increase in free time: legislation brought in the Saturday half day, the 10-hour Act, and early closing for shop workers.

Economics characterised by the systems of capitalism and industrial patronage led to the formation of works and church teams, which often developed into professional clubs. Sport had become part of the entertainment business and many entrepreneurs saw that money could be made from it.

The development of rationalised sport began in public schools and was spread by 'old boys', church men and school masters working in local communities. Active and manly recreational activities were seen as a means of social control, keeping both schoolboys and the working classes out of trouble while at the same time developing skills and virtues that would be useful to the ever-expanding empire.

Several factors affected the development of sport through the twentieth century. There was a steady move away from participation to the phenomenon of watching sport, initially through spectatorism but increasingly through the media. Spectatorism generated money, which led to professionalism in virtually all sports. Many sports performers are now full-time, paid entertainers.

What the examiners will expect you to be able to do

- Outline the development of sport after 1800.
- Explain the impact that changes in society had on the development of sport.
- Discuss the effect of the three key revolutions: industrial, transport and urban.

Tip The characteristics of sport in the post-industrial phase should be the opposite of those you identified for the pre-industrial phase. See if you can use the mnemonic you created for the pre-industrial phase to help you remember key points for the post-industrial phase of sports development.

The emergence of physical education

Key points

- Sport as a means of social control within nineteenth-century public schools.
- Development of sport within the Oxbridge university system and its diffusion throughout Europe and the British empire.
- Development of PE in state schools (elementary) during the twentieth century:
  - the Forster Education Act, making education compulsory in 1870
  - adoption of European systems of gymnastics from Germany and Sweden
  - the increasing influence of Madame Osterberg
  - the effect of the Boer War, resulting in the introduction of the Model Course and the dominance of military PT
  - then follows a struggle for influence between the military, education department and the medical boards
  - the 1933 PE syllabus
  - the effects of the Second World War and its influence on modern PE
- Current and future policies in school sport and PE.

Sport in English public schools during the nineteenth century

Organised games began to appear in public schools (attended by boys from the upper classes), at first as spontaneous recreations and for the most part disapproved of by the teachers. However, as the games became more developed it was recognised that educational objectives could be passed on through participation in games. Sports became a feature of all public schools, with team games forming the central core. The main sports were football and cricket (and rowing at schools situated near rivers). These games were physically strenuous and demanding. They relied on cooperation and leadership — all characteristics that a gentleman needed to acquire.

In 1827, Dr Thomas Arnold became headmaster of Rugby School. He was to have an important influence on the reform of public schools. Although Arnold's main concern was the education and control of his pupils, the programmes and rules he introduced had a parallel effect on the reform of games and sports in schools.

Arnold's main innovations were to introduce:
- the house system, which led neatly to the formation of early sports teams
- prefects, who organised the games and activities of the boys — the first administrators
- 'muscular Christianity' — the idea that there is a close link between Christianity and the concept of sportsmanship
- a philosophy of character — games were soon seen as a vehicle for personal development

The success of schools such as Rugby led to the cult of games spreading throughout the private education system. The Industrial Revolution created a new affluent social class (the middle class), resulting in a huge market for private education. Middle-class families wanted their sons to be educated as gentlemen and to service this need there was a huge increase in the number of preparatory schools. The prominence of games and sports was further enhanced with the publication of the Clarendon Commission report in 1864. The Commission's role was to investigate the management and programmes of the nine great public schools. The nine schools identified in the report were Charterhouse, Eton, Harrow, Rugby, Merchant Taylors', St Paul's, Shrewsbury, Westminster and Winchester.

The impact of athleticism on society

The development of sport through the public school system of the nineteenth century had a profound effect on the spread of sport throughout society, both in Britain and the British empire. It sowed the seeds of rationalisation, in which sports were codified and regulated by governing bodies. The boys who left the schools spread the cult of manly games across the world.

An effective way of memorising this impact is the mnemonic CAT PUICCA.
- **C — colonial**. Many former public school boys took up posts in the colonial service, helping to administer and govern the empire's colonies. They took with them their sporting kit. Initially they played among themselves, but gradually introduced the sports and games to the indigenous populations.
- **A — army**. Another career for many old boys was as commissioned officers in the armed forces. Initially the officers used sports as a recreation to fill the long hours, but the social control and moral value of keeping the working-class soldiers occupied were not lost on them. This played an important part in spreading the cult still further.

- **T — teaching**. Many former pupils became teachers, especially in the now expanding preparatory and grammar schools. Often they simply repeated the programme of games and physical recreation they had followed in their school days. It was not unusual for sporty teachers at the end of the nineteenth century to play for the school teams.
- **P — patronage**. Supporting sporting events and competitions, for example by providing funding for trophies or land for pitches, was another important role undertaken by old boys.
- **U — university**. This was a very important stage. Cambridge and Oxford (chiefly) gave young men further time and resources to pursue and refine sporting activities. One major problem, though, was the plethora of different rules for the various games. In order to allow everyone to play, compromise rules were required and this was the first step towards the rationalisation of sport.
- **I — industry**. Once they had finished school, many boys returned to their fathers' factories and businesses. These were Thomas Arnold's 'Philistines'. Their love of sport needed an outlet and soon clubs were set up which were linked to these factories. At first there were some social limits — only managers and office staff could join the teams — but gradually the lower classes were also admitted. Many current football teams — Stoke City, West Ham, Manchester United — were formed in this way.
- **C — church**. Much of the boys' education was based on religion, so it is not surprising that many took up careers in the church. Muscular Christianity promoted the use of sport as a vehicle for teaching morals and Christian virtues. Many clergymen used it in its most practical form, encouraging sports and setting up teams both here and abroad. Again there are examples in modern football — Aston Villa, Everton and Wolverhampton Wanderers have church origins.
- **C — clubs**. The first stage for many old boys was to form clubs so they could continue to play their games. The Old Etonians is a good example of this type of club, but there were many others formed.
- **A — administration**. When their playing days were over, many men joined governing bodies and developed their sports by helping to formulate national rules.

The development of PE in British state schools, 1870–1944

Physical education developed through stages:

drill $\longrightarrow$ physical training $\longrightarrow$ physical education

Modern PE grew from two main pathways:

- games from public schools, which aimed to develop character and leadership
- physical training from elementary schools, which was devised to develop fitness and discipline

The 1870 Forster Act made education compulsory, but there was limited development of PE due to lack of facilities and space. The two main influences on gymnastic development stemmed from two European countries:

- Germany, based on the work of Guts Muths and Friedrich Ludwig Jahn
- Sweden, based on the work of Per Henrick Ling

It was the Swedish system of 'drill', inspired by Ling, that had the biggest impact on the development of PE in Britain. Ling's system was adopted by many schools' boards — most importantly the London School Board, which appointed Madame Bergman Osterberg to oversee this implementation. She played a central role in the development of PE in Britain, establishing the first specialist teacher-training college at Dartford in 1895.

The first model course for PE in schools was written by the War Office in 1902, prompted by the poor health of recruits for the Boer War. This syllabus was revised with a different focus in 1904–19 and a modern syllabus, taking the best of physical training and introducing PE as a subject in school, was introduced in 1933.

Post-war educational philosophy led to a movement away from prescribed syllabuses. In 1952, the Ministry of Education published *Moving and Growing* and in 1954 *Planning the Programme.* All PE teachers received copies. These publications offered advice and suggestions rather than commands, and represented the final move towards a child-centred approach to PE.

Current and future policies in school sport

Even with the National Curriculum for PE, no one school's programme is the same as another's. In recent years, the academic study of PE has grown greatly and it is now studied at many levels. The National Curriculum identifies six sports activity areas: games, athletics, gymnastics, dance, swimming and adventure. Schools should offer pupils experience in at least five of these activity areas.

Recent initiatives in PE and school sports include the TOP sports programmes, sports college status and the development of school sports coordinator networks.

TOP Sports programmes

The TOP Sports programme has three key features:
- adapted sports-specific equipment that is child-friendly
- sports-specific illustrated resource cards to introduce sporting skills
- training and ongoing support for teachers

The following programmes are now available for schools and community groups to offer:
- **TOP Tots** — helping children aged 18 months to 3 years experience physical activities and games
- **TOP Start** — encouraging 3–5 year olds to learn through physical activity
- **TOP Play** — supporting 4–9 year olds as they acquire and develop core skills
- **TOP Sport** — providing 7–11 year olds with opportunities to develop skills in a range of sports
- **TOP Skill** — challenging 11–14 year olds to extend their sporting skills and knowledge
- **TOP Link** — enabling 14–19 year olds to take a lead in the organisation of sport
- **TOP Sportsability** — creating opportunities for young people with disabilities to enjoy, participate and perform in physical education and sport

THE HENLEY COLLEGE

Sports college status

Specialist sports colleges are one element of the UK government's specialist schools programme set up in 1997. By 2005 there were 250 secondary schools with sports college status in the UK. Schools have to bid for the status in a process that involves raising a considerable sum of money and proving their commitment to high-quality provision of PE and school sport. If it is successful, the school receives a grant from the government to improve its sports facilities and increase its staff team. For the next 3 years, the school receives additional funding to help support its role in developing sports excellence locally and widening participation among its partner schools.

School sports coordinators network

Sports colleges are integral to the school sports coordinator programme. This UK government initiative focuses on improving the quality and quantity of extra-curricular sport and inter-school competition.

The network is based around families of schools with a sports college at the centre. School sports coordinators, normally existing PE teachers, are given time away from lessons to help manage and coordinate sports fixtures and opportunities in their local schools. They also help to develop and extend programmes of sport in primary schools.

What the examiners will expect you to be able to do

- Discuss how sport was used as a means of social control in nineteenth-century public schools.
- Describe the development of sport within the Oxbridge university system and its diffusion through Europe and the British empire.
- Outline the development of PE in state schools (elementary) during the twentieth century.
- Describe the current and future policies in school sport and PE.

Tip Memorise the mnemonic CAT PUICCA to help you to remember how the public schools' sports system was spread across the rest of society (see pages 15–17).

Social influences on performance and participation

Key points

- Basic requirements for sport and recreation.
- Lifestyles in contemporary society.
- Concepts of access, opportunity, provision and esteem.
- Sociocultural factors affecting access.
- Geographical factors.
- Stereotyping and esteem.
- Concept of target groups and reformative policy.

Basic requirements

The basic requirements for sport and recreation include:

- fitness — a basic level of physical fitness
- ability — the skills needed to play sport
- resources — access to kit and equipment
- time — leisure time away from work and other duties

Lifestyles have changed over the last century — the development of transport and other technological advances have meant a move to a more sedentary lifestyle. Work and leisure often require much less physical activity than they used to. There are now concerns about the lack of fitness amongst young people and the rise of diseases such as obesity and cardiac problems.

Cultural factors

Many people do not have equal access to sport, often as a result of discrimination due to cultural variables. A number of so-called target groups can be identified. These are groups that consistently find it difficult to access sport and recreation. There are five main cultural factors that can lead to discrimination in sport:

- gender
- social class/economic status
- ethnicity (race and religion)
- age
- ability/disability

Discrimination can be said to affect the following areas in sport:

- opportunity
- provision
- esteem

Opportunity

There may be barriers to an individual's participation in an activity. In the UK, most sport takes place in clubs run on a voluntary basis, which are often elitist organisations. Clubs work on membership systems and membership is controlled either by the ability to pay the fees or, in cases such as some golf clubs, election to the club membership. This often limits membership to certain members of the community.

Another consideration for the individual is whether he/she has the time to play. Women in particular are frequently faced with this problem. The demands of work and family often mean that they have little leisure time, which accounts in part for the low levels of female participation in sport.

Provision

Are the facilities that allow participation available to you? Living in an inner-city area might discriminate against you because there is often little provision in these areas. Equipment is also required, which can be expensive. Those on low incomes may be discriminated against unless equipment is available free or can be hired cheaply.

Esteem

This is concerned with the views and judgements of society. In many cultures, societal values dictate that women should not take an active part in sport, or if they do it should be confined to 'feminine' sports such as gymnastics and not 'macho' pursuits such as football and rugby. These judgements are based on the traditional roles that men and women have taken in society and may be very difficult to break.

Stereotypes and sports myths

Stereotypes are assumed societal variables that lead to discrimination. Often minority groups within a community are labelled as having certain characteristics or traits, and this can lead to them being steered into certain sports or positions and away from others.

Stereotypes may lead to **myths** in sport, leading to discrimination. Common sports myths are that 'black people can't swim' and that 'women will damage themselves internally if they do hurdles'. Myths are based on very little truth, but often become an important aspect in selection and opportunity.

A good example in the UK is the current lack of Asian footballers. Much research has been done in this area and programmes are now being set up to try to redress the imbalance. The main problem is that, in our societal view, Asians are not potential footballers.

Stereotypes and myths can become self-fulfilling prophecies. Even the people they discriminate against may believe they are valid and conform to the stereotype by displaying their appointed characteristics and choosing the sports that fit them. In doing so they are reinforcing society's view. It is only recently that sports centres have begun to attract older customers, many now run programmes such as 'ageing well' in an attempt to persuade more people that an active lifestyle can have health and fitness benefits throughout life.

Geographical factors

Geographical factors can also affect the opportunity of access to sport and recreation. Where a person lives and the distance to facilities and natural resources will affect their decision regarding which sports to take up and how often they should participate. Some areas of the UK have large areas of natural resources, such as beaches and lakes, which facilitate recreation. For those who live in a city there may be parks and open spaces to use and they may have easier access to built facilities. However, they may have a long way to travel to partake in outdoor recreations.

Educational factors

Most people first learn to play sport at school and consequently the type of school and PE experience a person has been through can affect their choice of sport and recreation in adult life. School facilities are now opened up after school and at weekends. The current government policy of extended opening will happen in every school across the country, which means that more people will have access to sports facilities.

What the examiners will expect you to be able to do

- Describe the basic requirements for sport and recreation.
- Comment on lifestyles in contemporary society.
- Explain the concepts of access, opportunity, provision and esteem.
- Discuss how sociocultural factors affect access.
- Explain the concepts of stereotyping and esteem.
- Discuss the concept of target groups and reformative policy.

Tip Look for local examples of target-group programmes and reformative policies at your local sports centres. Don't forget to use these in your examination answers.

Professional (elite) sport

Key points

- History of the development of professional sports.
- The role of the national governing bodies of sport in the UK.
- The role of European and international sports bodies.
- The nurture of talent in the UK.
- The concepts of commercialisation and Americanisation in UK sport.

The structure of sports organisation in Europe

In all EU member states, sport is traditionally organised in a system of national federations or governing bodies. Only the top federations are linked together in European and international federations such as UEFA and FIFA. The structure resembles a pyramid.

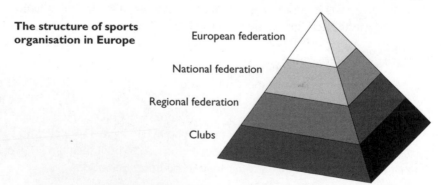

The structure of sports organisation in Europe

European federation

National federation

Regional federation

Clubs

National governing bodies of sport

Most modern sports developed their present form within the last 150 years. As participation in sport began to increase at the end of the nineteenth century and many activities became popular, it became necessary for those taking part to agree to a common set of rules. Until this time there had been regional variations and it was very difficult for teams from different schools or areas to play against each other.

This need for **codification** led directly to the formation of a governing body within each sport. The main role of a sports governing body was to harmonise rules and develop a national pattern of organisation. It is for this reason that the rules and organisation of each individual sport in the UK lie in the hands of an autonomous national governing body. Each body is responsible for the general administration of the sport and the conduct of competitions.

The foundation of the system is that clubs become affiliated to their particular governing body. Clubs pay a fee to become members of these bodies, which gives the club the right to vote on sports issues and to take part in competitions.

At present there are over 300 national governing bodies in the UK. Their major roles are to:
- establish rules and regulations
- organise competitions
- develop coaching/leadership awards
- have direct responsibility for sport at the local and national level, as well as representing the sport in international matters
- select teams and competitors to represent the home countries or the UK at international events

Elite sport

Excellence in sport can have two meanings: elitism, which means 'all for the best — forget the rest'; or optimum performance, where everyone has the chance to succeed.

Most societies emphasise elitism, as this produces champions. There is much diversity in the methods of nurturing talented athletes used by different societies.

An elite sports model

In elitism, the emphasis is on a few — the best performers. The tendency is to look for the most developed and ignore the rest. The best example was seen in the former German Democratic Republic, a country with a population of only 16 million, which managed to be in the top three for sports such as athletics, swimming and boxing. The whole system of sports in this communist country was geared to selecting and developing champion performers, but this was at the expense of the rest of the population. The sports facilities and coaches were only available for the elite athletes, and there was little or no provision for the rest of the population.

The development of excellence

There are three key stages in the development of sporting talent:
- selecting talent
- developing talent
- providing support for performance

The actual methods used to develop talent differ from country to country but, increasingly, similar policies are being followed by most. Many of these have been adapted from the eastern European model of sports excellence, pioneered by the Soviet Union and the German Democratic Republic from the 1950s onwards.

Selection

The development of excellence begins with selection — identifying individuals with the potential to become champions. The pyramid theory of sports development suggests that the wider the base, the greater the number at the top of the pyramid. The aim of the selection process is to make the base of the pyramid as wide as possible.

Talent development

Stage two is again a crucial aspect. The children selected are coached, instructed and nurtured to become champions. In many countries, this process is achieved through the education system, predominantly in sports schools.

Sports schools are found in most European countries and are often controlled by the state. They allow young people to develop their sporting potential while continuing with their academic studies. They usually have high-quality facilities and specialised staff, the advantage being that students get more time to practise their skills and the atmosphere of excellence encourages their development.

Providing support for performance

The final part of the process is to provide support in terms of administration and funding. In many countries, the state funds the top athletes. In Australia and France (as in the old Soviet Union) all top performers are paid grants that allow them to become virtually full-time athletes. In America, talented performers are paid scholarships by schools and colleges, or are contracted to a professional team. In the UK, SportsAid tries to fund up-and-coming athletes. As yet there is little government input to sports in the UK.

Modern sports performers also require the support of an ever-increasing range of sports specialists — psychologists, dieticians, physiotherapists — as well as video and computer equipment to help improve technique. In the UK, such services are now being developed in a number of national sports centres, forming a national network with the UK Sports Institute (UKSI) as the central focus. The aim is to enable our international performers to use top-quality facilities for training. These now come under the Sports Council's World Class Performance programme, funded by the National Lottery. This sports fund has three levels:

- World Class Start — programmes aimed at developing talented youngsters.
- World Class Potential — assisting the development of teenagers and helping with educational support.
- World Class Performance — supporting our elite athletes both financially and by providing top-class facilities through the UKSI.

The funding of UK sport is prioritised to ensure the most effective use of lottery funds and to achieve the overall aim of the UK being one of the world's top five sporting nations.

The UKSI network centres, alongside the FA football academies and specialist sports colleges, provide lifestyle management training and support for talented young performers. Most of this is carried out through the Athlete Career and Education (ACE UK) programme. ACE UK provides a tailored service that encourages elite athletes to take control of all aspects of their lives. It enables athletes to identify their personal strengths and helps them to integrate career, education and sporting demands so that they can be successful now and in their life after sport.

The ACE UK programme is modelled on the ACE programme developed through the Australian Institute of Sport. It is a national programme delivered regionally through the UKSI network in order to promote accessibility.

All elite UK athletes undergo an individual athlete assessment with a local adviser in order to identify their needs and introduce them to the wide range of support ACE UK has to offer. This could include financial management support, workshops on media training or access to the Olympic and Paralympic Employment Network (OPEN), which helps athletes in employment with training and work demands.

Americanisation and commercialism in UK sport

Sport is now seen as big business and in order to compete and develop, sports increasingly turn to the private sector for finance. This system of funding through sponsorship and media fees first developed in American sport and has now crossed the Atlantic in a process referred to as 'Americanisation'. This move to private funding has also changed the main ethic in sport from the traditional recreational ethic of playing for the love of the game (an amateur focus) towards a more commercial 'win at all costs' attitude. This has brought a move towards an 'open' focus where performers are free to earn money from their sport. The Rugby Union's move towards a professional premiership in the late 1990s is a good example of the way traditional amateur sports have become more Americanised.

What the examiners will expect you to be able to do

- Outline the history of professional sports development.
- Explain the role of the national governing bodies.
- Discuss the roles of European and international sports bodies.
- Discuss the nurture of sports talent in the UK.
- Comment on the development of commercialisation and Americanisation in UK sport.

Tip See if you can reproduce the organisation pyramid for your own sport. This might make it easier for you to remember the key stages in your examination.

Recreative sport (mass participation)

Key points

- The European Charter and its link to the concept of Sport for All.
- The role of national agencies in the promotion of sporting activity.

- Grass roots programmes in sport.
- Concepts of target groups and reforms.
- Amateur sport and the voluntary sector.
- The rise of wilderness and adventure sports.

Grass roots

This is the lowest level of the participation pyramid, where the masses are encouraged to take part in active pursuits. This sector is dominated by amateur performers who do not receive many rewards for playing sport. It is also referred to as the voluntary sector as the people that help organise and run the sports do so in their own time. Sport is a natural part of life, whether you are one of the elite competing for gold medals or just playing for enjoyment. The opportunity to take part in sporting activity should be a basic human right. However, many people suffer constraints that prevent them from taking part. The aim of mass participation is to break down these constraints, whatever they may be, and to encourage as many people as possible to take up sport. The Sports Council estimates that only one in three people in the UK regularly takes part in sport.

The Sports Council

The Sports Council has four main aims:
- to increase participation in sport
- to increase the quality and quantity of sports facilities
- to raise standards of performance
- to provide information for and about sport

In 1994 it was announced that the Sports Council would be reshaped to create two new bodies: the UK Sports Council and the English Sports Council, rebranded as Sport England in 1999. This brings England in line with the other home countries in that it now has its own sports council. The UK Sports Council has a coordinating role, ensuring that all councils work in the same direction, and has responsibility for drugs testing and doping control in all UK sport.

Each council is split further into regional and local sports councils, enabling area-specific planning. Funding comes from the National Lottery sports fund and Sport England receives £200 million per year. This money is used to run the regional councils, fund campaigns and capital projects (e.g. building new facilities) and provide information services. However, most of it is redistributed to sports governing bodies and institutions as grants to be used for increasing sports participation, building new facilities and setting up recreation programmes.

The Sport for All campaign

The Sport for All campaign, originally set up in 1972 and still continuing, highlights the value of sport and promotes the idea that sport should be accessible to all members of the community. The campaign initially hoped to increase the opportunities for sport and recreation through developing more facilities, and by educating the public on what is available. More recently, the campaign has diversified to target groups of the community that remain under-represented in sport. Campaigns such as '50+ and All to Play For' (aimed at older people) and 'What's Your Sport?' (aimed at women) have followed.

Sport for All in Europe

The concept of Sport for All first emerged in the early 1960s in Germany and the Nordic countries. In 1968, the Council of Europe initiated the setting up of several projects aimed at encouraging mass participation. Their stated aim was 'to provide conditions to enable the widest possible range of the population to practise regularly either sport proper or various physical activities calling for an effort adapted to individual capacities'.

The growing interest in sport and in the specific development of Sport for All by all European countries led to the adoption of the European Sport for All Charter in 1972. This asserted that 'every individual has the right to participate in sport' and that 'it is the duty of every member state to support financially and organisationally this ideal'.

The main organisation charged with implementing Sport for All has been the Committee for the Development of Sport (Comité Directeur pour le Développement du Sport), known as the CDDS.

The performance pyramid

The different levels of sport can be represented best as a pyramid. Such a concept is used by many sports organisations to develop a continuum of participation from grass roots to elite. In theory, the broader the base of participation, the greater is the elite pool from which a society can select.

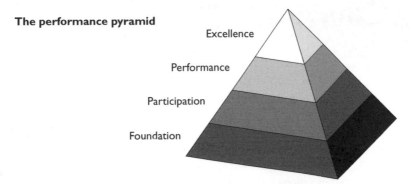

The performance pyramid

Excellence

Performance

Participation

Foundation

Tip It may be easier to revise if you use examples from the sport you play when referring to the different levels of the sports pyramid.

There are four levels of performance within the pyramid:
- The **foundation level**, also known as the grass roots level, is mainly associated with young children being introduced to sport and learning the fundamental motor

skills. In the UK, schemes such as TOP Sport and Dragon Sport have been used by the sports councils to promote participation at this level.

- At the **participation level**, older children are beginning to play full-scale sport, often for teams based in school or the community. The School Sports Coordinators programme and the Sports Education and Step into Sports initiatives are examples of strategies used to encourage participation at this level.
- The **performance level** is associated with participants who are committed to performing in formal, organised competition at higher club and regional level. Participants will usually train for their chosen sport and be members of a local sports club or organisation.
- The **excellence level** is where elite athletes perform at a national and/or international level. For many of these performers, sport is their main focus or career. They receive funds either as professionals or through grants and awards from sports organisations such as the Sports Lottery Fund.

What the examiners will expect you to be able to do

- Explain the European Charter and its link to the concept of Sport for All.
- Describe the role of national agencies in the promotion of sporting activity.
- Identify and describe grass roots programmes in sport.
- Discuss the issue of target groups and suggest reforms.
- Describe in detail amateur sport and the voluntary sector.
- Explain the rise of wilderness and adventure sports.

Tip Many of the issues and points in this section of the unit relate to those in the section headed 'Social influences on performance and participation' (see pp. 19–22). It may be useful to revise these two areas together.

The Olympics Games

History and philosophy

Key points

- The Games of the ancient world and the influence they have had on the structure and philosophy of the modern Games.
- The founding of the modern Olympic Games by Pierre de Coubertin and the influences of the English public school system, amateurism and the myth of the recreational ethic
- De Coubertin's motives and philosophy for establishing the modern Games.
- The development of the Games through the twentieth century and the way they have adapted to reflect the new ethics in sport.
- How the Olympics are awarded and why cities want to host an Olympic Games.
- The history and role of the Paralympics.

The modern Olympic Games

The first modern Olympic Games were held in Athens in 1896. They were founded by Baron Pierre de Coubertin, a French aristocrat. He had studied the ancient Olympics, but drew most of his inspiration from the English public schools.

The Olympic Charter is the codification of the fundamental principles, rules and bye-laws adopted by the IOC. It governs the organisation and operation of the Olympic movement and stipulates the conditions for the celebration of the Olympic Games. The first Games in 1896 attracted 245 athletes (all men) in 43 events. At the Athens 2004 Games, more than 11099 athletes from 202 countries took part in 218 sports.

The Olympic symbol, the five interlocking rings, represents the union of the five continents and the meeting of the athletes of the world at the Olympic Games. The plain white background of the Olympic flag is symbolic of peace throughout the Games.

When the modern Olympic Games began in 1896, **amateur status** depended as much on social class as it did on being free from the so-called professional taint of earning money from sport. De Coubertin had simply adopted the public school 'recreational ethic'. The early Olympic competitors were gathered from the elite of European and American society since they had to pay their own way to the Games. Many athletes in various sports found themselves in a difficult situation over the question of their amateur status.

The pressure of being able to train and compete at the highest level made its demands in terms of time and expense. This led to the concept of **shamateurism**, which in turn led to a change in emphasis in sport with the 'win ethic' replacing the 'recreational ethic'.

To many performers, sport had become a career rather than a leisure pursuit. Commercial pressures increasingly permeated all sports. Entrepreneurs saw the commercial possibilities of having their products identified with popular sport. By 1981, the IOC had removed the term 'Olympic amateur' from the Olympic Charter.

Bidding

Bidding to host an Olympic Games now takes place 7–8 years before the actual year of the Games. Each Olympic nation can put forward one city. These are scrutinised initially by the national Olympic committee and then by the IOC before a shortlist of five is produced. An IOC commission visits each bidding city and reports back to the IOC members, who then vote on which city will host the Games.

Since the commercial success of the 1984 Los Angeles Olympics, and because of the increasing profits that can be made from hosting a Games, up to 40 cities now begin the bidding process. In the late 1990s, there were accusations of corruption. For example, Salt Lake City was accused of paying IOC members to secure votes. An official review was undertaken, some IOC members were fired and new, tighter rules were introduced regarding the gifts and the hosting of IOC members visiting bidding cities.

The Paralympic Games

Paralympic means parallel to the Olympics. The Games motto is 'Mind, body and spirit'. The Paralympic movement began life in 1948 as an organised sports competition for veterans of the Second World War who were suffering from spinal cord injuries. The opening day of that first competition coincided with the opening day of the 1948 London Olympic Games. However, it was not until 1960 that a Games on the Olympic pattern was first organised. It was a further 16 years before the competition was expanded to include other disability groups at the Toronto Games in 1976. The Games for the disabled were initially held as an independent event, but have shared the main Olympic venue since the 1988 Games in Seoul.

It was not until 1988 that a commitment was made by the full Olympic Organising Committee to assist the **International Paralympic Committee (IPC)** with the organisation of the Games. The Paralympics represent the pinnacle of achievement in disability sport. As the movement itself has grown, the number of athletes involved has increased from 400 in 1960 to just over 3500 in Athens 2004.

What the examiners will expect you to be able to do

- Explain how the Games of the ancient world influenced the structure and philosophy of the modern Olympic Games.
- Discuss how de Coubertin was influenced by the English public school system, amateurism and the myth of the recreational ethic.
- Discuss de Coubertin's motives and philosophy for establishing the modern Games.
- Outline the development of the Games through the twentieth century and the way they have adapted to reflect the new ethics in sport.
- Explain how the Olympics are awarded and why cities want to bid to host an Olympic Games.
- Describe the history and role of the Paralympics.

Tip Your answer should always start with an introductory paragraph outlining how you are going to answer the question set. It may be useful to revise and pre-write part of this paragraph and then adapt it to the question set in your examination.

The Olympic issues

Key points

- Race and ethnicity within the Olympic movement, including the positive and negative effects participation in the Games by ethnic minorities has on participation globally.
- The growth of commercialisation at the Olympics and the move away from the founding amateur philosophy. The reforms of Peter Ueberroth and the creation of the TOP sponsors scheme.
- Women within the Olympic movement — from zero participants in 1896 to around

a third at the turn of the twenty-first century and the link to the wider societal image of women.

- Political uses of the Olympics as a means of gaining global recognition for a country or cause. Examples of systematic protests, such as boycotts and propaganda, and non-systematic protests such as the Black Power demonstration in 1968.
- Deviance in the Olympics — reasons and methods, the move away from the original concept of sportsmanship towards the new, commercially oriented idea of gamesmanship. The key problem of drugs in sport and the IOC's role in international drug control.

Race and ethnicity

It has long been part of the Olympic ideal that athletes should be free to participate in the Olympic Games irrespective of race, colour or creed.

In the early years of the Olympics the events were dominated by white Europeans and North Americans and it is only recently that athletes from other cultures and races have appeared in numbers at the Games. There is still much concern about the continued white dominance of positions within the IOC. This reflects the theory of centrality, which suggests that the dominant roles in sport are held by people in the dominant sections of the society in which the sport is played.

Generally participation by different races is seen as a positive move since it creates role models which can inspire another generation of athletes from those races. However, the theory of stacking suggests that there may be a negative effect in that ethnic minorities are often channelled into certain sports. This may be due to stereotypes and myths which develop, suggesting that particular races are more suited to specific events and sports.

The growth of commercialism within the Olympic movement

In the past, the Olympics were used to promote all that was good in sport. All competitors were amateurs competing purely for enjoyment, and although the winner received a medal, it had no monetary value. However, as the modern Games moved into the second half of the twentieth century, television especially opened up a huge global audience. This had the effect of making the Games very attractive to commercial sponsors, but also gave nations, groups and individuals a world stage on which to make their point.

Media and sports funding

The presence of the media has turned sport into a commodity that can be bought and sold. Television companies pay huge amounts of money to cover sports, and advertisers and sponsors back sport because of the exposure they will get in the media. Individuals train and prepare for sport in the knowledge that the media will give them a stage on which to present their talents — and also gain wealth.

There is a direct link between the funding of sport and the media. Media coverage brings sponsors and advertising to sport, which are now essential for a sport to remain viable. Companies sponsor sports mainly as a means of cheap advertising — a way of getting into the public's living room. This is referred to as sport's 'golden triangle' and is becoming increasingly essential in the success of sports events. However, recent European legislation is due to phase out all tobacco sponsorship in the next few years.

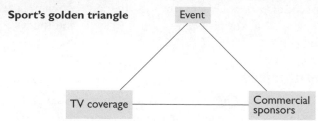

Sport's golden triangle

For some more peripheral sports, such as hockey, a vicious circle exists. To attract sponsors you need media coverage, but to gain this coverage you need the funds to attract top performers and make the sport more popular with the media.

The influence of the media, and specifically television, over sport is epitomised by the Olympics. This great event is controlled by American television companies, who pay well over $400 million for the exclusive rights to screen the Olympic Games. This kind of financial influence gives the companies control over many factors. For example, we are now used to having to stay up very late to see key events such as the 100 m final, so that it fits with the prime time television slot on the east coast of America.

Gender issues

Much of the early reluctance to allow women to compete at the Games was due to de Coubertin's philosophy. His opinions on women and sport were influenced by the model of the ancient Greek Games. There were no women at the ancient Games, either as competitors or spectators, and when de Coubertin revived the modern Games in 1896 he upheld this feature. Women did compete at the 1900 Games, but only in tennis and golf. The opening of the track and field events to women at the 1928 Games was highly significant. Annoyed at the refusal of the IOC to include women's athletics in the 1924 Games, a French woman, Alice Milliat, threatened to set up a rival women's organisation. This caused the IAAF (International Association of Athletics Federation) to step in quickly and endorse women's athletics. The IOC responded by including athletics for women in the 1928 Games, which put women's sport at the centre of the Olympic and world stage.

By 1936 there were still only four sports available to women, but gradually the number of women competing and the number of events open to them has increased.

In the 1970s, changing attitudes towards women in society meant that it became acceptable for the sporting female to be attractive. A host of female athletes such as Olga Korbut, Nadia Comaneci and Nelli Kim became household names and helped to promote female participation in sport.

Beauty and grace are still almost unavoidably associated with many women's sporting activities. This, of course, is a societal trait rather than an Olympic one, but it does mean that sports that portray feminine qualities tend to receive more attention and coverage.

In the Athens 2004 Games there were 28 sports and 116 events for women; however, there were still twice as many male competitors as there were women.

Although female participation in the Games is increasing, membership of the IOC is still very much dominated by men.

Political use of the Olympics

The Olympic Games generate a huge media and spectator following which creates a shop window for both the performers and the nations they represent. This has meant that many have used the Games to make political protests. At one extreme states have not allowed their athletes to compete in order to make a political point aimed at other competing nations. This is known as a boycott and the games of 1956, 1976, 1980 and 1984 were severely affected by boycotts. The Games have also been used in a more positive way. In 1964 South Africa was excluded from the Games because of its policy of apartheid (a system of government which discriminated against the black population). It was only when this system was abolished that South Africa was finally allowed back into international sport in 1992.

Berlin, 1936

The first Olympic Games where politics was openly evident were held in Berlin in 1936, which became known as the Nazi Olympics. Berlin had been awarded the Games in 1931, but by 1936 Adolf Hitler's Nazi party had taken over Germany, and Hitler wanted to use the Games to show the world how powerful Germany and its people were.

Hitler believed in the supremacy of the Aryan race ('true' Germans — blond-haired, blue-eyed and muscular): they would dominate the Games and show that the German race was superior to all others. Unfortunately for Hitler, a young black American athlete called Jesse Owens dominated the Games, winning four gold medals. Owens was the only athlete not to receive his gold medals from Hitler, who left the stadium in disgust. Three years later, Hitler's aggression led to the start of the Second World War.

Mexico City, 1968

Two main problems affected the 1968 Olympic Games. Mexico was a very poor nation and many people felt that the huge amount of money needed to host the Games would have been better spent helping to develop the country. Mexican students held a number of demonstrations in opposition to the Games, the final one being 10 days before the Games were due to begin. Over 10 000 people marched to the Square of the Three Cultures in Mexico City. Aware of the impact such a demonstration could have in the world's media so close to the start of the Games, the Mexican authorities reacted strongly, sending in the army to surround the demonstrators. A fierce battle developed, in which 260 people were killed and several thousand injured. Amazingly, the Games went ahead with no further trouble.

The next political problem occurred within the Olympic stadium. In America in the late 1960s, black civil rights groups had been protesting about the lack of opportunity for black people and the racist attitudes in American society. With the world's media watching, two young black American athletes used the medal ceremony to show their support for the Black Power movement. In the 200m final, Tommie Smith took gold and John Carlos took bronze. As they stood on the medal podium listening to the American national anthem, they bowed their heads and each raised one gloved hand in the Black Power salute. Both were expelled by the US Olympic Association and sent home immediately.

Munich, 1972 — the terrorist Games
During the Games in Munich, Palestinian terrorists stormed part of the Olympic village, taking several Israeli athletes hostage. There had long been a serious disagreement between Palestinian groups and the Israeli authorities over the ownership and control of disputed land. The German police attempted to stage a dramatic rescue but it went wrong. Nine athletes, a policeman and five terrorists died. Many felt that the Games should be abandoned in honour of the athletes killed, but the IOC decided to carry on — to show, they said, that no terrorist group could stop the Games.

Montreal, 1976
There were two main problems associated with the Montreal Games. The Canadian Government underestimated the costs and ran out of money before all the facilities were completed. In fact the Canadian people are still paying via their taxes for the 1976 Olympics. After this, the IOC allowed more commercial companies to be involved in the Games to provide financial backing.

The Montreal Games were boycotted by several African countries, which were unhappy that New Zealand had been allowed to compete in the Games even though their rugby team had continued to play against South Africa.

Moscow, 1980
Boycotts dominated the Games in Moscow in 1980. In December 1979, the Soviet Union had invaded Afghanistan. The USA, Canada, West Germany, Japan and Kenya did not attend the Games in protest.

Los Angeles, 1984 — 'tit for tat'
Because the USA had led the boycott of the Soviet Olympics in 1980, the Soviet Union led a boycott of the 1984 Games in Los Angeles. No Eastern bloc countries competed in these Games.

Seoul, 1988
The Seoul Games were dominated by the feud between the political systems of communism and capitalism. Korea is a divided country, the north being a communist state, the south capitalist. Seoul (in South Korea) was awarded the Games by the IOC,

but North Korea applied to stage some of the events. The IOC refused and North Korea and three other communist countries boycotted the Games.

In 1988, professional athletes were allowed to compete for the first time, so ending another Olympic tradition. This was mainly to do with the inclusion of tennis as an Olympic sport.

Barcelona, 1992
The Barcelona Games were a success. There were no boycotts and through the development of the commercial side the Games made a profit. South Africa was allowed back into the Olympic movement after abolishing apartheid. The Soviet Union was replaced by the Commonwealth of Independent States, and West and East Germany were joined as one team.

Atlanta, 1996 — the centenary Games
Atlanta will be remembered for the hype and glamour, a terrorist bomb and the organisational problems that hindered athletes and spectators alike. Many people felt that the centenary Games should really have gone back to Greece, home of both the ancient Olympics and the first modern Games, but the IOC chose Atlanta. Atlanta is the home of Coca-Cola, the Olympic movement's biggest sponsor.

The Americans claimed that these would be the best Games ever, but problems with transport systems and the very hot weather led to many complaints. The lowest point of the Games was a terrorist bomb exploding during a music concert for athletes and fans in Centenary Park. It killed several people and injured many others.

Sydney, 2000 — the best ever
This was perhaps the most successful Olympic Games. Sydney provided excellent organisation and venues coupled with the support of the Australian public. Extensive security and the isolation of Australia meant there were no incidents to report. There was concern over athletes using performance-enhancing drugs, but the Sydney authorities were determined to crack down on drug abuse and began testing athletes in their training camps. This resulted in 43 athletes testing positive and being sent home before the Games began.

Athens, 2004
Although conflicts continued around the world, at the Athens Games there were no boycotts or threatened terrorist attacks, no one used the Olympic podium to make a protest and the team from Iraq received a standing ovation when it entered the stadium at the opening ceremony.

Deviance and the Olympics

All sports have rules and deviance occurs when participants break these rules. This **cheating** is an important issue in modern sport.

Cheating is not a new concept — we know that the ancient Olympians took tonics to try to improve their performances. Some people would argue that cheating is an important element in sport and that without it sport would be dull.

Sport has many written rules but there are also unwritten ones, and these make investigation of deviance more complicated.

The concept of sportsmanship

The Olympic ideal is based around the philosophy of **sportsmanship** — people conforming to the written and unwritten rules of sport. The idea of **fair play** means that you treat your opponents as equals and, although you want to beat them, you will do so only by adhering to the rules and a code of conduct that has been developed in the sport through tradition. This includes shaking hands and congratulating the other team or opponent at the end of the game. Cheating not only destroys the game but also detracts from your personal achievement. A win through cheating is a hollow victory where you may gain the extrinsic rewards, but not the more fulfilling intrinsic ones.

Gamesmanship

The alternative dynamic in sport is known as **gamesmanship** — where you use whatever means you can to overcome your opponent. The only aim here is to win, and for most people it is not a question of breaking the rules, but more bending them to their advantage.

Drugs in sport

Drug abuse has been one of the main areas of deviance in sport over the last few years. It is not clear whether the actual level of drug taking has increased or whether we are now more aware of it because testing systems have improved. It is also difficult to decide where the line should be drawn between illegal and legal substances. Many athletes have tested positive but claim that they only took cough mixture or other such products that can be obtained without prescription.

What the examiners will expect you to be able to do

- Discuss the issue of race and ethnicity within the Olympic movement.
- Explain the growth of commercialisation at the Olympics and the move away from the founding amateur philosophy.
- Discuss the role of women within the Olympic movement.
- Explain and discuss how the Olympics has been used as a means of gaining global recognition for a country or cause.
- Discuss the issue of deviance in the Olympics.

Tip Always include a plan at the start of your answers to this section of the exam paper. Your plan should include an introductory paragraph and a definition of key terms. Work through parts of the question, get examples/chronology in order and check that you are answering the question set. Include a concluding paragraph that sums up your answer.

THE HENLEY COLLEGE

Questions & Answers

This section contains questions similar in style to those you can expect to see in your Unit 1 examination. The limited number of example questions means that it is impossible to cover all the topics and all the question styles, but they should give you a flavour of what to expect. The responses that are shown are real students' answers to the questions.

There are several ways of using this section:

- Hide the answers and try the questions yourself. It needn't be a memory test — use your notes to see whether you can make all the points you need to.
- Check your answers against the candidates' responses and make an estimate of the likely standard of your response to each question.
- Check your answers against the examiner's comments to see if you can appreciate where you might have lost marks.
- Check your answers against the terms used in the question — did you *explain* when you were asked to, or did you merely *describe*?

Examiner's comments

All candidate responses are followed by examiner's comments. These are preceded by the icon 🅔 and indicate where credit is due. In the weaker answers, they also point out areas for improvement, specific problems and common errors, such as lack of clarity, weak or non-existent development, irrelevance, misinterpretation of the question and mistaken meanings of terms.

Question 1

Concepts and definitions

Comment on the differences between sport and recreation and suggest how a sports facility might accommodate both these concepts.

(6 marks)

Total: 6 marks

■ ■ ■

Candidates' answers to Question 1

Candidate A

In general, sport is classed as an activity played professionally and as a competition with a set structure. Sport accommodates assets such as opponents and brings about competition, ultimately ending with a winner and a loser. It is played with set, formal rules governed by some form of referee and must be played within boundaries. In contrast, recreation is a more freely performed activity. It is done for personal satisfaction and enjoyment (intrinsic rewards). No opposition is required and competition is minimal. Rules are informal and there are no set boundaries. Recreation is a very individual activity.

Sports facilities are generally open to the majority of the public and offer opportunities for both sport and recreation. Many clubs (e.g. rugby, football, tennis) are designed for sporting activity. Other clubs, such as gyms and leisure centres, are mainly for recreational use. They provide areas for people seeking enjoyment.

Candidate B

Sport is competitive — you play against an opponent and there will always be a winner and a loser. This is different from recreation, because recreation is non-competitive. There are generally no rules for recreation — if there are they are informal. There are no officials. Sport is played for intrinsic and extrinsic rewards, whereas recreation is done for intrinsic reward — for self-satisfaction.

A sports facility could accommodate these differences by having set times and spaces for the two different types of activity. Competitive games and activities, such as tournaments, can be arranged. In terms of recreation, non-competitive drop-in sessions could be arranged. Trophies or prizes could be given as extrinsic rewards for sport, but recreation would be played just for enjoyment — an intrinsic reward.

🖉 This question requires candidates to answer in two parts — initially explaining the differences between sport and recreation and then going on to discuss how a sports facility might accommodate both these concepts. In terms of mark allocation, examiners would expect a minimum of three points for each part of the question. Candidates could only score a maximum if they answer both parts of the question fully. Candidate A scores well on both sections, explaining the differences and going on to give examples of how a sports centre can accommodate both activities. Candidate B also provides enough points for both parts of the question. Both candidates score 6 marks.

Question 2

Combat sports in pre-industrial Britain

Discuss the importance of combat sports in Britain before 1800. Use examples to support your answer.

(5 marks)

Total: 5 marks

■ ■ ■

Candidates' answers to Question 2

Candidate A

Before Britain underwent industrialisation, combat sports were considered the only real activity and essential sport. Before the 1800s, there were many wars and invasions affecting Britain. The country saw that in order to maintain a strong defence and flexible attacking skills, it was vital for the masses to practise and become experts in combat — they would be prepared for any event.

Two main types of combat sports were practised. One was jousting, which provided military training for the upper classes. The other was archery, and it was compulsory for the lower classes to practise every Sunday after church. The main reason for this was because there was plenty of room for practice in the churchyard, and the trees from which the bows were made were also found there.

Candidate B

Combat sports were very important in Britain before 1800 as they kept the men fit for war and gave them the various skills needed in battle. It was compulsory to do sports such as archery; the King gave the order that every man had to practise. If people failed to do so, they would be punished.

The upper classes took part in combat sports to show the public how important and how high up they were in society. An example of this type of combat sport is jousting — you received points for attacking your opponents; the more hits you made, the more points you received. This sport also helped to develop horsemanship skills, which knights would use in battle.

Archery is another example of a combat sport. It was compulsory for every man to own a bow. Archery practice and competitions would take place after church on Sundays. There would be many spectators and prizes for the best shots.

The public schools of the nineteenth century introduced games for both educational and social reasons.

e Both candidates make a good attempt at answering the question set and give a range of examples in their answers as requested. Candidate A makes a number of points and backs up the examples with explanations, but does not make enough to score all the marks available. Candidate B gives good detail and scores enough points to match the marks available. Candidate A scores 4 marks, while candidate B scores the maximum 5. Other points to make could include the need for self-defence skills and how combat was used to settle arguments and feuds in the pre-industrial age.

Question 3

Sport in nineteenth-century public schools

(a) How were games used as a means of social control in public schools?   (3 marks)

(b) Identify elements of the 'games tradition' established in schools such as Rugby during the nineteenth century, which still exist in many UK secondary schools.   (4 marks)

Total: 7 marks

■ ■ ■

Candidates' answers to Question 3

Candidate A

(a) The games practised, such as football, were useful as a means of social control because they aided in the development of personal sportsmanship and responsibility. Students were given the idea of enjoyment and the responsibility for learning as a team. Games were used to develop social skills that could be used later in life. Students passed on these sports to other areas of society. For instance, those students who went on to be priests or went to university passed on the rules. Sports in public schools were played throughout the British Empire and produced students with honourable characteristics, creating good soldiers for the army.

(b) The elements of the games tradition that are still evident consist of the many attributes that games created in the nineteenth century. These games developed students into responsible and fair men.

Candidate B

(a) Games were used as a method of social control within public schools because it taught the boys how to work as a team. Games such as rugby, cricket and football were used as character-building methods of social control. Within these games boys had to adhere to set rules and regulations which helped to develop discipline. Public schools were looking to produce leaders. The games required exercise and stamina which would benefit the boys both within school, by allowing them to channel their energy, and in the wider society.

(b) Elements of the 'games tradition' that still exist in schools now include prefects. Prefects were established in schools during the nineteenth century to organise the games and make sure everybody knew their role. Sport as an education also developed from public schools. It was seen as an important part of learning and started to be played in many other schools. Inter-school competitions were introduced, where schools competed against each other to see which one was best. This also happened within schools, between the different houses, and the idea of house matches is still evident in many modern schools.

e This question focuses on the popular exam area of public school sport. In the first part candidates need to explain the term social control. Both candidates make a good attempt. Candidate A makes a number of valid points relating to character but misses the main point of sport being used as a means of channelling aggression and energy. The first part of the question scores 2 marks, but no marks are awarded for part (b). Candidate B makes a range of points, including the key point about games channelling aggression and energy. Named sports examples are given and 3 marks are awarded for each part of the question. In part (b) candidates need to think about their own high school and use examples that link back to the games tradition. These could include house teams and competitions, the role of prefects and house captains and the awarding of school colours to students who play in teams.

The effects of the Industrial Revolution

What changes in British society led to the rationalisation of sport in the late nineteenth century?

(4 marks)

Total: 4 marks

■ ■ ■

Candidates' answers to Question 4

Candidate A

The industrialisation of Britain led to more spectators in sport and more leisure time in which to take part. Rules started to be established in most sports. Games played in school now had one set of rules. This was because the students could read and write and therefore rules could be used.

Candidate B

The effect of the Industrial Revolution led to many changes in sport. Urbanisation led to people having less spare time to participate in sport because they were working longer hours. There was not much land available because of all the factories and buildings. Sports were also wagered upon, especially by the upper classes who did not participate in sports themselves. Transport was beginning to develop and become popular. This meant that the upper classes could move out of the city to participate in more rural pursuits such as walking and hunting. For the working classes it meant that teams could begin to travel to compete against teams from other areas. Rules now had to develop so that teams could play to standardised versions. The setting up of compulsory education in 1870 aided this as it meant that everyone could now read and write and therefore understand the new rules.

This is a good example of the need to read the question carefully. The question clearly asks students to make points relating to changes in society. Candidate A shows some knowledge of the development of sport in this historical period but fails to answer the question set. Only the last part regarding the development of education can be given 1 mark. Candidate B, on the other hand, makes a number of valid and correct points and does answer the question set, scoring the maximum 4 marks.

The administration of sport in the UK

Discuss the role that national governing bodies (NGBs) play in the organisation of sport in the UK.

(4 marks)

Total: 4 marks

■ ■ ■

Candidates' answers to Question 5

Candidate A
NGBs register the teams that play in their sport's leagues and competitions. They fund their sport by raising money. They organise the leagues and competitions. NGBs also devise rules and change the rules for their sport.

Candidate B
The role of the governing bodies in sport in the UK is huge. Their duties include:
- setting up, maintaining and amending the rules of their sport
- implementing disciplinary procedures against players and teams that break the rules
- organising national competitions, for example the FA Cup
- developing and administering coaching awards and qualifications for their sport
- selecting and coordinating the training of the national team for their sport

e Here we have a difference in answer styles, and both are acceptable in this section of the exam. Candidate B uses bullet points, which is acceptable as long as each point makes sense. This style is useful because it can help candidates to make sure they write enough different points to match the marks available. The answers would have been better if the candidates had made reference to a specific governing body. Much of the information for this answer will have been covered in your local and national provision assignment. Both candidates score the maximum 4 marks.

Factors affecting participation

Sport for all is not yet a reality in the UK. How can a person's opportunity to participate in sport be affected by sociocultural factors?

(5 marks)

Total: 5 marks

■ ■ ■

Candidates' answers to Question 6

Candidate A

- Age — as you get older, it is harder to get to facilities due to the costs of transport, for example.
- Gender — women find it more difficult to access sports due to problems related to time and money.
- Race and religion — these may restrict a person from taking part in sport or recreation, e.g. Muslim girls may not be able to take part in sports such as swimming or gymnastics.
- Disability — some leisure centres cannot accommodate disabled people, e.g. they don't have ramps or disabled changing facilities.
- Economic status — people with less money cannot afford to participate in sport because in the UK we have to pay to play.

Candidate B

The age of the individual can affect his or her access to sport. The very young and the old find it more difficult to access sport and recreation. Where people live can also affect their access to sport. Those who live in rural areas may find it difficult to get to sports clubs. The ability of the individual can also be a factor, as can the fitness of the person. A person's gender is another factor — boys and girls play different sports.

e Again there is a difference in answer styles. You can see clearly that Candidate A makes at least five references to sociocultural factors and backs up each point with explanation and/or examples. This answer would score the maximum 5 marks. Candidate B does score some marks as he/she does attempt to identify five factors, but fails fully to explain them or back them up with examples as Candidate A does. In this type of question it is beneficial to put down one or two extra points if possible, to ensure that you score maximum marks.

Question 7

Politics at the Olympics

How have the Olympic Games been used by governments and individuals for propaganda purposes?

(25 marks)

Total: 25 marks

■ ■ ■

Candidates' answers to Question 7

Candidate A

The Olympic Games have been used by governments for political propaganda since the Berlin Games in 1936 when Hitler wanted to show the world his ideas on white supremacy. This attempt at propaganda was ruined by Jesse Owens, a black American who won four gold medals. Hitler ignored Owens at the medal ceremony and failed to accept this dent in his theories.

At the Melbourne Games of 1956, conflict over the Suez Canal led to two nations, Egypt and Lebanon, attending the Games as both felt participation by officials and athletes may give the other country an advantage in the war.

The 1968 Mexico Games were also the scene of political protest. This began even before the Games were opened. Many people felt a developing country like Mexico, with financial problems and high levels of poverty, should not be wasting money on hosting the Games. Many individuals and groups protested in the streets of Mexico City and were harshly treated by the fascist government. Over 200 demonstrators were killed in the protests.

At the same Games, a new form of propaganda was seen for the first time. Athletes used the Olympic podium as a stage to demonstrate about their political and civil beliefs. Two black American sprinters gave the Black Power salute during the playing of the US national anthem. This was in protest at the USA's historical role in the black slave trade. The relay team repeated the protest when they received their medals and all the protesting athletes were sent home and stripped of their medals for using the Olympic arena for political protest.

China has also used the Games for political gain. It refused to compete in the same Games as the Taiwan team and withdrew from several Olympic Games and the IOC altogether for many years.

When Moscow was awarded the 1980 Olympic Games, many countries disapproved because of the Soviet Union's poor record on human rights. This was manifested when the Soviets invaded Afghanistan at the beginning of the Olympic year. Many Western countries, led by the USA, refused to attend the Games. In Britain, the decision was left up to individuals and most athletes stated that sport should be above politics and they should not waste an opportunity to attend the Olympic Games. The Soviets spent much time and effort developing strong male and female teams so they would beat the other nations, so proving their superiority. Since then, many other countries, such as France and the USA, have used sport to show off their country. In the 1984 LA

Olympics there was another boycott led by the Soviet Union. This became known as the 'tit-for-tat' boycott.

At the Barcelona Olympics of 1992, South Africa was allowed back into the Games because the country had abandoned its policy of apartheid. Apartheid, where black and white people were segregated, had led to other countries banning South Africa from the Olympic movement as a show of solidarity against racism. This began when many African nations boycotted the Montreal Games because New Zealand was allowed to take part despite having played rugby union against South Africa.

For many years after the Second World War, East Germany used political propaganda in its bid for honours at the Olympic Games by not allowing drug testers into the country.

I think the Olympics should return to their ideal roots, which Baron de Coubertin had in mind when he launched the Games at the end of the last century. He felt the Games should be pure and not about money, sponsorship or commercialism. Instead of talking about political point scoring, we should report on the success of the athletes. However, the scale and global nature of the Games do lead to propaganda. People like the Black Power sprinters knew millions of people were watching them; television companies pay millions of dollars for exclusive rights to beam the Games around the world. Globalisation means that people around the world can see the protest and the point it is making. Sportsmen and sportswomen have the power to change the way people think and to fight against injustice — an example is Jesse Owens in 1936.

Candidate B

The Olympic Games have been used by governments and individuals for propaganda purposes many times. The Olympic Games were originally developed as a sports person's event and had nothing to do with warring nations. When the Olympics first began in about 776 BC they ran for over 1000 years without missing one, even if nations were fighting. The Olympics brought the nations together.

The Games were brought back in 1896 by Baron de Coubertin. They have run to the present day, missing only three because of world wars — in 1916, 1940 and 1944. But the Olympic Games have been used by people to protest and boycott. For example, in the 1936 Olympics in Berlin, before the Second World War, Hitler was in power in Germany. Many people disagreed with these Olympics because of Hitler's ideals and policies on Jewish and black people. Jesse Owens, a black American, won four gold medals, but Hitler refused to present them because Owens was black.

The Moscow Olympics were also used by governments for propaganda. The USSR had invaded Afghanistan and all the governments that had control over their athletes banned them from attending the Games in protest. However, some countries did not have power over their athletes. Many of these athletes said sport should be above politics and attended the Games.

There was an individual protest by athletes at the Mexico Olympics in 1968. Two black American athletes who won medals raised their fists on the podium when the national anthem was played, in protest about the black slave trade. This was known as the Black Power salute and was repeated at other Olympics.

e Both candidates have produced direct answers. Neither has produced a structured answer and both need to add an introductory and a concluding paragraph. Candidate A has produced a very detailed answer with a wide range of specific examples. The question is answered using points relating to both governments and individuals. The answer is perhaps a little too descriptive and does not really explain how the Games are used for propaganda purposes. This answer is about the right length, but needs more planning and structure. Candidate A scores 16 marks for this answer. Candidate B's answer is shorter, though it still manages to give a range of related and factually correct examples from various Olympic Games. Again there is limited explanation and no real discussion about the issue of politics and propaganda. This answer would also benefit from more planning and structure. Candidate B scores 14 marks.

Women at the Olympics

Often society's view of women is reflected within the world of sport. Women feel compelled to conform to a set image referred to as 'femininity'. Discuss how women's position within the Olympic movement reflects this statement. (25 marks)

Total: 25 marks

■ ■ ■

Candidates' answers to Question 8

Candidate A

Plan:

- 1896 — de Coubertin's view — no female competitors
- 1900 — some female events — more in 1904
- Alice Milliat — influential
- Sporting stars — Blankers-Koen/Olga Korbut/Paula Radcliffe — no marathon until 1992
- Sports myths — stereotypes — Olympics affect mass participation
- 1968 — television — fashion
- 2004 still fewer women's events — no hammer throw

De Coubertin believed that the only job of women in a sporting arena was to present the garlands to the winning male athletes and this was reflected in 1896 when women were forbidden to compete. However, by 1900 women were allowed to compete in a few events such as tennis and archery and by 1904 the number of events for women had increased again.

In 1928, Alice Milliat threatened to stage a women-only Games in opposition to the Olympic Games. This threat led to women being allowed to compete in more events during the mid part of the twentieth century.

During the Second World War, a lot of women had to take jobs that the men had left behind. Women showed that they were capable of doing the work of the men and this helped lead to a large increase in the number of events women were allowed to compete in after the war. Fanny Blankers-Koen showed her ability when she won four gold medals, which was considered a great achievement in the world of female sport.

In 1968, television coverage of the Games was born and one of the first female stars to attract the attention of the media was Olga Korbut. She showed that the sporting female could also be attractive and this led to the media wanting to promote this image. Events such as synchronised swimming and gymnastics became very popular among female participants and fashion came to play a large part in female competitions.

However, because women's events were now more about fashion and femininity, a lot more women believed that it was the way they looked, rather that their sporting ability, that attracted the attention of the media. This view also led to the formation of certain sports myths such as women can't throw, or women may damage internal organs if they compete in the hurdles. These beliefs still affect people at mass participation level wanting to take up certain sports. A lot of women believe that they need to have a set image and a certain amount of femininity and by not having this they cannot play certain sports or take part in the events they want to.

In 1992, women were allowed to run the marathon for the first time and this has helped to produce stars such as Paula Radcliffe. This is a positive step away from stereotypes and sports myths and also shows that women are capable of participating in events that were considered to be male only.

However, there are still fewer events for women in today's Olympics. For example, women are still not allowed to compete in the steeplechase or the hammer throw. This problem leads to the Olympics being seen as male dominated. The situation is improving though and nowadays the emphasis is more on how females perform in a sporting sense rather than on how they appear in a fashion and glamour sense.

Candidate B

In 1896, Baron de Coubertin set up his Olympic dream for the modern Games. In it he stated that the role of women in the Olympics was not to take part, but to bestow garlands upon the heads of the winners. Such a view of exclusion from participation for women was very much reflected by their position in the wider society.

Women were undervalued in society and were thought to be inferior to men. Their role historically has been to stay at home and look after the needs of the family, not to go to work or war. Women were considered to be too weak and this perception has been hard to shake off. This meant that women developed a very low self-esteem when thinking about sport. Many felt that sport was too competitive for them and did not reflect the image of femininity. In the first modern Olympics there were no events for women and thus no female competitors. This reflected the society of western Europe at the end of the nineteenth century.

The stereotype of women began to change as the twentieth century developed. Despite de Coubertin's ideals, at the 1900 Games held in Paris, 20 women took part in two sports — tennis and golf. They were now being allowed to participate, but only in sports that were stereotypically right for them.

Until 1920, women competitor numbers increased, but these were still hugely inferior to the number of males in the Olympics. Alice Milliat took a stand against this discrimination and decided to form a Women's World Games in direct competition with the Olympics. The International Olympic Committee (IOC) was worried that this would harm the growing reputation of the Olympic Games and decided to allow more female sports and competitors into the Games. Milliat's women's games were scrapped, but she had won an important battle and one that reflected growing emancipation in the wider society. Around the same time, the suffragettes had managed to get the right to vote for women in England.

The view of women in sport and society continued to improve. At the 1948 Games held in London, the number of sports for women had increased to 21 and there were now 385 female athletes competing. However, this was still far lower than the number of male athletes at the Games.

In 1981, the IOC selected its first female member, showing a continual improvement in the view of women in sport and work. By the Atlanta Games (1996) there were 97 different events for women to compete in compared with 161 events available to male competitors. This shows that the female stereotype is continuing to be broken and the set image of femininity applies much less than when the modern Olympics began. Women are viewed better both by themselves and others, encouraging them to participate more in sport and the Games. Factors such as positive stereotypes and female role models are reasons behind such change. Figures such as Olga Korbut and, more recently, Kelly Holmes at the 2004 Athens Olympics have encouraged women at grass roots level and those closer to the elite level to participate and strive for success.

The IOC has the ability to make changes that will further change attitudes to women in sport and at the Olympics. They could encourage participation by showing more coverage of female events, possibly leading to more role models for young women to emulate. They could encourage all the member countries to do more for female sport at all levels. The IOC has also said that '…by 2006 we hope that 20% of the IOC representatives will be female'. This is another positive step that will help raise the view of women. Finally, they could put women on an equal footing with men by offering the same number of sports and events in the Olympic Games. This would instantly present a view to the world that women are seen to be equal to men in sport and especially in the Olympics.

In conclusion, I have discussed how the participation of women in the Olympic Games has improved dramatically since 1896 and this reflects their improving status in the wider society. However, women are still seen to be inferior to men in the Olympics and there are fewer female athletes at the Games, fewer events in which they can compete and fewer female IOC members. The IOC can address this problem to further enhance the view of women and encourage more women to get involved in sport.

✎ Candidate A has produced a sound descriptive essay with evidence of planning and some structure. It is full of relevant examples and moves along well, giving an in-depth account of the rise of women as performers at the Olympic Games. However, it makes only limited links and reference to women in the wider society and makes no points about the other roles that women could play in the Olympic movement. It does develop some analysis of the issues of femininity within female sport. This answer scores 17 marks. Candidate B's essay scores slightly higher marks because it makes more links to the wider society, as asked for in the question. This answer also has a good structure, although there is no evidence of planning. The candidate makes good use of practical examples to back up the points made — some are very contemporary, relating to the most recent Olympic Games. This answer scores 18 marks.

Amateurism at the Olympics

In 1896, the modern Olympic Games were established around the principle of the 'amateur ideal'. Discuss whether this principle is still relevant to Olympic performers in the twenty-first century.

(25 marks)

Total: 25 marks

■ ■ ■

Candidates' answers to Question 9

Candidate A

Plan:

- Before — amateur — 'love of sport' — professionals banned — de Coubertin's ideals — public school athleticism
- After twenty-first century — drugs/deviance — professionals allowed — drive to win — political system — use politics to prove something

Many of the principles around which the modern Olympic Games were established are still relevant in the twenty-first century. However, as time has passed, many changes in the structure and issues within society have taken place and these are reflected in the Olympic Games of the twenty-first century. The principle of the amateur ideal primarily means the love of sport and although many athletes may still feel this, there are many influences that now go against de Coubertin's established 'amateur ideal' and 'Olympic dream'. In this essay, I will outline the meaning of the amateur ideal and discuss the similarities as well as the differences that exist in relation to this view in the twenty-first century.

The modern Olympic Games, established by Baron de Coubertin, were very much a celebration of sport. Competitors took part because of their love and enjoyment of their sport. The amateur ideal prevailed in that competitors did not receive any extrinsic rewards for their performances. Those who played for money or other extrinsic rewards were banned from competition at the Olympics. De Coubertin wished for the Games to allow equal opportunity for everyone. He wanted the qualities he recognised and admired in the British public schools to be reflected in the attitude of the competitors at the Games. He wanted every athlete to abide by the rules and acknowledge the concept of fair play. Perhaps most significantly, he stressed that the Olympic Games would not be an opportunity for political control. All these ideals were, of course, impossible due to the changes that were to occur socially, financially and politically during the twentieth century.

The Olympic Games of the twenty-first century now fully support the idea of professionalism. The amateur status of the modern Olympics rarely exists and competitors receive money from sponsors and grants from government and sports organisations. This is accepted because of the time athletes now have to spend training and preparing. An Olympic athlete needs to train full time for most of the

year and there is no possibility of being successful at the Olympics and continuing to have a job. Although the change from amateurism to professionalism has occurred, many athletes still compete for the love of their sport and not merely for the rewards that come with it.

Deviance in the Olympics is one of the aspects that counteracts de Coubertin's amateur ideal. For many athletes, the success of a win has become more important than taking part. Therefore, in many respects, the concept of sportsmanship has now been replaced by gamesmanship. Many athletes will do anything to win, including tampering with equipment and taking banned drugs.

Politics has inevitably become part of the Olympics, with many countries using the Games to show their superiority. For example, the many boycotts of the 1970s were to prove political points — often that a country did not want to be associated with another one.

The many changes that have taken place in the time from the re-emergence of the Olympic Games in 1896 to the Olympics of the twenty-first century go against the principles of the amateur ideal. However, the love of sport and desire to participate still exist along with those athletes who still practise good sportsmanship and show the honour that comes with competing for one's country.

Candidate B

The modern Olympic Games still function around the amateur ideal; it is arguable that most of the athletes are 100% amateur. However, the boundaries are constantly being stretched through sponsorship and funding, along with the amount of media coverage the Olympics now enjoy.

The athletes who compete at the Games are not actually paid, but receive grants and scholarships from governments or lottery funds. These grants provide funding for the athletes to buy their own training equipment. They can also be used to provide adequate housing, food and supplies.

High-profile athletes may receive sponsorship deals from big brand names such as Adidas or Nike. These companies, as well as providing specialist equipment, tend to stretch the boundaries of what they provide for their athletes, and this brings into question whether the athletes are actually being given the same benefits as professionals. Some sponsors provide luxuries such as cars and other expensive gifts.

All this challenges whether the principle of the amateur ideal still exists. Another challenge to the amateur ideal is the increasing role the media play in modern sport. Virtually all athletes who compete at the Games receive media coverage. This may mean that athletes are used in advertising features in the same way as professional athletes. Moreover, the fact that they appear at the Games alongside professional performers raises the question as to whether they can still be labelled as amateur athletes. Stars such as Paula Radcliffe, Matthew Pinsent, Steve Redgrave, Jonathan Edwards and Colin Jackson have been projected through the media frequently and no doubt have been able to secure huge sponsorship deals as a result of all the media coverage.

On the other hand, most athletes try to remain low profile. Although they are at the elite level, they do not receive direct payment to compete and so the amateur ideal still exists. It is true to say that receiving sponsorship deals and supplements is not against the rules, and many athletes would do the same if put in a similar situation. The amateur ideal does still exist in the twenty-first century. Athletes go about their way of life in a professional, elite manner, but this is not reflected through any types of structured or one-off payments. The fact that many receive subsidies is just a reflection of current society. For most athletes these grants, which are still well below the average annual salary, mean that they can train and prepare for their events. Most of them will only get one attempt at the Olympics and will then have to return to a normal job and lifestyle.

🖉 Candidate A has written an essay that broadly answers the question set. The answer starts off with a good discussion about the concept of amateurism. What it lacks is any real depth or factual examples to back up the points made. The answer follows a sound structure and includes both an introduction and a concluding paragraph. Candidate A scores 14 marks. Candidate B answers more directly and sticks to the point well. This essay is not as well structured and again lacks sufficient examples to back up the points made. However, it does discuss the issues well and raises a number of original thoughts. Candidate B scores 15 marks.

History and founding philosophy of the modern Olympics

The formation of the International Olympic movement in 1896 was modelled around a blend of ancient and modern philosophy. Discuss and explain how this blend was reflected in the organisation and focus of the Olympic Games. (25 marks)

Total: 25 marks

■ ■ ■

Candidates' answers to Question 10

Candidate A

When Baron de Coubertin reintroduced the Olympic Games in 1896, they were based around the structure and philosophy of the ancient Games. De Coubertin wanted to follow a similar structure and range of events. Events such as javelin, discus and long jump were present at both the ancient and modern Games, forming a link between the two eras.

The Olympics were not only formed to allow countries to compete against each other in sporting rivalry, but also to encourage peace between all the countries in the world. However, this has not always been the case. Throughout the twentieth century there were numerous occasions when the Games were hijacked by nations and individuals in order to put forward political and nationalistic views. For example, in 1936 the so-called Hitler Games were used as a way of demonstrating Nazi power in Germany. The boycott by the African nations of the 1976 Games due to issues over the continued sporting links with South Africa further demonstrated the lack of harmony.

Whether it was de Coubertin's intention or not, the bidding process for hosting the Olympics has led to a change in values of the Olympics themselves. Participation at the Games is still a major draw for all countries, but since the 1984 Los Angeles Games the financial benefits of hosting the Games have developed.

The Olympics are still used by countries around the world as a form of shop window. By this I mean that countries use the Games to show the rest of the world how good they are in comparison. The simple pride and honour in hosting the Games has somewhat disappeared and money has taken over from the values of the early Games.

The Games themselves were intended to help nations (and individuals) to gain a sense of belonging and identity. As in ancient times, the Olympic Games are not an annual event but are held every 4 years. These Games were designed in general terms to help all continents to gather in one place. They were seen as an attempt to discourage the wars that were rife around the world during the nineteenth and early twentieth centuries, hoping to prevent conflict by allowing nations to participate and compete with each other in sporting activities. A good example of this is the case of the Cold War between the USA and Russia. The Games, rather than open conflict, were used by each nation in an attempt to prove which was the better country.

Many would say that the Olympics are a shadow of what they used to be when they were formed in 1896. But although the sports may have changed somewhat and the number of events increased, the real underlying philosophy behind the Games that de Coubertin introduced still exists.

Candidate B

Baron Pierre de Coubertin was born in France in 1863. While growing up he became fascinated by the world of sport and education. In 1889, de Coubertin organised a conference to discuss his views on education and sport. After the conference he received a note from Dr Penny Brookes, inviting him to the Much Wenlock Games to see how sport was used to bring people together in friendly competition. De Coubertin was much impressed and during this visit he decided to visit a number of public schools that he had read about.

His most important visit was to Rugby School, where headmaster Thomas Arnold had introduced a programme of muscular sports. De Coubertin was impressed with the British attitude to sport and education and he truly believed that other countries, such as his native France, could learn from and emulate the British and hopefully also achieve military and political greatness, as Britain had with its empire.

The notion of athleticism is based on Christian virtues and values. This was a code of conduct for public school boys so that they would grow up into future leaders and learn the norms and values of society through playing sports and games such as football and rugby. These norms and values included loyalty, obedience, honour in defeat and, most importantly, fair play. This was known in public schools as Muscular Christianity.

De Coubertin believed that it was these ideas that had built the British empire into the success it was. From this he developed his Olympic ideal. He wanted to bring the ancient Games back and bring all the nations together to participate.

In 1896, de Coubertin's dream was brought to life when the first modern Olympic Games took place in Athens. Thirteen nations and 133 athletes competed. The nations included Austria, Australia, Britain, Italy, USA, Germany, Hungary, Greece and France. There was one Italian man who possessed the true Olympic spirit — he walked all the way to Athens, but was told on arriving that he was too late.

However, de Coubertin's Olympic dream was far from fulfilled. He had resurrected the ancient Games, but only to a certain extent. The Games themselves were a reflection of the society of the time. Participation at the Olympics was only allowed if you were classified as a gentleman. This meant being born into wealth and money and you were not classed as a gentleman if you were employed by another person. Competitors had to pay for their own travelling.

At the time, women were seen to be unable to participate in the Games purely on the basis that there were no women in the ancient Games. This also reflected what was happening in society. Women had to conform to the set image of femininity.

Other reflections include d race, because admission was controlled by the White Anglo Saxon Protestants (WASPs) power group. People of colour were unable to participate, based on the fact that they were at the bottom of the social class scale.

In conclusion, the Olympic Games were controlled, and participated in, by the upper end of the social scale, which was a true reflection of the time. The gentry controlled everything. Hence it would be some time before de Coubertin's dream of all people from all backgrounds participating in the Olympic Games was fulfilled.

Candidate A has produced a sound answer that is well structured and moves along well. The essay makes a range of valid points and backs up nearly all these with practical examples from various Olympic Games. This answer also shows a degree of originality, especially towards the end where the candidate gives a personal opinion on the issue. Throughout the essay, Candidate A refers back to the question, ensuring it is answered, and so avoids reproducing a pre-planned answer. Candidate A scores 19 marks. Candidate B manages to develop some structure, but strays a little from the question set. The answer starts off well with some good historical points but then gets bogged down with the issue relating to class. There is no real development of the point about the Games being used to bring the world together in peace. Candidate B does include a concluding paragraph and scores 14 marks.